Contents

Changing times

These pictures show children in
the present and in the past.

You are growing up
in the present.

Present
This is a
school today.

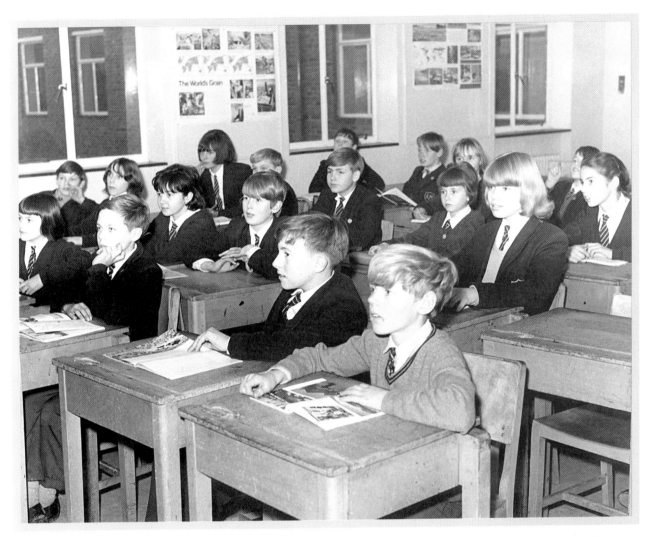

Your mum grew up in the past. Many things have changed since your mum was a child.

In this book, lots of different mothers remember what it was like when they were your age.

Past
This is a school in 1964.

Record player

"When I was little, we played music on a record player. We used to sing and dance to our favourite songs!"

The records were made of a hard plastic called vinyl. You had to be careful that they didn't scratch or break.

Playing clackers

"When I was little, my favourite toy was my clackers. The idea was to make the balls bump into each other so they made a clacking noise."

Whoever gets ten clacks in a row wins.

It took practice to make the plastic balls bump together.

Twin tub

"When I was little, I helped my mum wash the clothes in a machine called a twin tub. It had two tubs. The first one did the washing, then we put the dripping wet clothes into the second tub to spin."

There was a
hose to fill the
twin tub with
water from the
kitchen sink.

Kathakali

"When I was little, I lived in India. Every year, we went to see the Kathakali dance. We sat in the front so I could see the dancers up close."

Kathakali dancers wear colourful costumes and makeup. They act out exciting stories.

Colour TV

"When I was little, I saw a colour television for the first time. The picture was very bright — much brighter than a black-and-white TV. It was strange to see my favourite shows in colour!"

The first colour TV show in Britain was a tennis match from Wimbledon in 1967.

Holiday abroad

"When I was little, we went to Spain on holiday. I was the first person in my class to fly on an aeroplane or to visit a different country. It was very exciting!"

Travelling abroad was a new experience for most people in the 1960s and 1970s. Holidays to hot, sunny countries became popular.

Wearing a poncho

"When I was little, my gran knitted me a poncho. It spun out like a fan when I twirled round! I thought my poncho was groovy. 'Groovy' was one of my favourite words."

Ponchos were first worn in Mexico and South America.

Sugar cane

"When I was little, we grew sugar cane plants in the yard of our house in Jamaica. It was my job to water them. The water bucket was very heavy!"

Sugar comes from the stems of the sugar cane plant. It is used to make foods sweet.

23

The Silver Jubilee

"When I was little, we had a big party to celebrate the Queen's Silver Jubilee. We ate sandwiches and jelly and waved our flags in honour of the Queen."

The Silver Jubilee in 1977 marked 25 years since Queen Elizabeth II became queen.

Riding a bike

"When I was little, my dad taught me to ride a bike. At first, he held me steady. Then he let go and I was riding all by myself! Now that I'm a mum, I'm teaching my own daughter to ride a bike."

Timeline

This timeline shows the years from 1960 to 2010.

1960

1970

1980

1990

2000

2010

During the 1980s and 1990s, these mums were young grown-ups.

During the 1960s and 1970s, the mums in this book were children.

You are a child now. What year were you born? When do you think you will be grown up?

Memories

Ask your mum about when she was a child. Ask your teachers and other grown-ups about their memories, too. Here are some questions to ask.

> What kinds of clothes did you wear?

> How was your school different from mine?

> What were your favourite toys and games?

> What special events do you remember?

> What things do we have now that you didn't have when you were a child?

Glossary

Memories   Things you remember from the past.
Do you have *memories* of your last birthday?

Remember   To think of the past.
Do you *remember* what you did yesterday?

Past   Time gone by. The *past* can mean yesterday
or it can mean a long time ago. Your mum was
a child in the *past*.

Present   Now. Today is in the *present*. You are a child
in the *present*.

Timeline   A chart that shows the passing of time.
See the *timeline* on page 28.

Index